# Jesus:
# God and Man

**Brian Sherring**

**ISBN: 978-1-78364-446-9**


**THE OPEN BIBLE TRUST**
**Fordland Mount, Upper Basildon,**
**Reading, RG8 8LU, UK.**

**www.obt.org.uk**

Small superscript numbers in the body of the text refer to end notes found in Appendix 3

# Jesus: God and Man

## Contents

Page

# Preface

# Preface

The apostle Paul writing to the Philippians, said, "I want to *know Christ* and the power of his resurrection and the fellowship of sharing in his sufferings" (3:10). The Scriptures encourage us to learn *about* Him, but this is just the first step towards Paul's great desire – 'to *know* Him'. The Lord's gentle rebuke to Philip was, "Don't you *know* me, Philip, even after I have been among you such a long time?" (John 14:9). It is one thing to read about somebody, quite another to meet them and know them on a personal basis. And so in writing this booklet I was concerned that it should not become just a theological study of technical detail, but hopefully a means of bringing all who read it closer to the One about whom Thomas confessed, "My Lord and my God!" (John 20:28).

Our knowledge of Him must of course be based solidly on Scripture. Other people's answers to the question, "What think you of Christ?" may be interesting; it is what the Scriptures say of Him that is of prime importance, for they "speak of Him". It is by reading and studying the Word of God, that we learn more of Him (John 5:39,40; Luke 24:27). The Being and nature of Jesus Christ is not a subject for the debating platform, so just as Moses took off his sandals in the presence of the Lord because the place where he stood was holy ground (Exodus 3:5) so should we, as we consider this most holy of subjects.

Whilst most people have no difficulty in accepting Jesus Christ as a man, some seem to have problems with believing that He is God. I would therefore be dishonest not to make my own position clear at the outset. I have been firmly convinced for many years of the Deity of Christ and I believe that this is what the Scriptures teach.

So this will not be a booklet of arguments for and against that belief, or a negative condemnation of those who do not hold my views. I will endeavour to set out what the Scriptures actually say of Him and readers must make up their own minds.

Just as faith without works is dead (James 2:17) so to study the nature and Being of Christ purely from an academic point of view cannot stand by itself. To our *knowledge* of Christ as God and man must be added the practical response of our *acknowledgement* of Him as Lord. And this will be reflected in the way we conduct our everyday lives.

# Part 1:
# The Man
# Christ Jesus

# Part 1:
# The Man Christ Jesus

## This Same Jesus

As Peter and the other Apostles stood on the Mount of Olives looking up into the sky where the Lord had disappeared behind a cloud at His ascension, two "men" dressed in white suddenly stood beside them and said, "Men of Galilee.... why do you stand here looking into the sky? **This same Jesus**, who has been taken from you into heaven, will come back in the same way you have seen him go into heaven." Very shortly after this event, Peter, standing up with the Eleven Apostles on the Day of Pentecost, proclaimed, "Therefore let all Israel be assured of this: God has made **this Jesus**, whom you crucified, both Lord and Christ."[1]

A man from Nazareth named 'Jesus', a fairly common name in New Testament times, had undergone the disgrace of crucifixion, died and risen from the dead, had ascended into heaven and "this same Jesus" would one day come back "in the same way" and to the same place, the Mount of Olives, in accordance with Old and New Testament prophecies. **This Jesus** God "made.... both Lord and Christ". Stephen, testifying before the Sanhedrin, "looked up to heaven and saw the glory of God, and **Jesus** standing at the right hand of God". We do not know whether Stephen ever saw Jesus the Christ during His earthly ministry, but he had no doubt now whom he saw; it was not a spirit, it was "Jesus", "the Son of Man".[2]

Many years later, Paul wrote in Romans of "**the one man**, Jesus Christ" (5:15) and in his first letter to Timothy, reminded him,

"There is…. one mediator between God and men, **the man Christ Jesus**" (2:5). He states this as a *present*, not a past fact. Even "the resurrection of the dead comes **through a man**. For as in Adam all die, so **in Christ** (the second **man**) all will be made alive" (1 Corinthians 15:21,22,45-47). And God has "given proof" that **this same man** will one day "judge the world with justice … by raising him from the dead" (Acts 17:31).

The implications of continuing to refer to Christ Jesus as 'the man', even after His ascension to the right hand of God, prompts interesting questions. In what way has He continued to be a man? And what is the nature of His resurrection body, His body of Glory? (See Appendix 1 re - what the Scriptures reveal of the resurrection body of Christ.) F.F. Bruce in his *Commentary on The Epistle to The Hebrews*, referring to the expression, "in the days of his flesh" (5:7 lit.) wrote:

> An expression which emphasises the conditions of human weakness of which He partook during His earthly life **and which does not imply that His incarnate state was terminated with His exaltation to the right hand of God.** If the expression did have this meaning (i.e. that His incarnate state was terminated at His ascension), it would seriously weaken our author's argument that Christians have **right now** a high priest who feels for them and with them in all their temptations and sorrows. (My brackets and emphases.)

Even when Christ, as High-priest, entered into the presence of God, "once for all by his own blood", to sit at God's right hand, He preserved no less His humanity than the Jewish High-priest of old when he entered the typical sanctuary on earth (Hebrews 9:7-28). In order to continue to be "a High priest", a "Mediator" between

God and men and the future Judge of mankind, He is still "**the man** Christ Jesus". He has not abdicated His human side and been absorbed in some vague spiritual sense into the Godhead: He remains man's representative, "an advocate with the Father, Jesus Christ the righteous" (1 John 2:1 *KJV*).[3]

This may prompt the question, "How can He be a 'man' (in the sense in which we understand that term) and yet sit at the right hand of God?" The relationship between the human and the spiritual is at present beyond our ken. Christ's present 'mode of being' is part of 'the mystery of Christ' not yet revealed, but we do know He has not abdicated His 'humanity'.

## Jesus: Truly Man

Whilst we may not yet understand the relationship between the human and God-ward sides to Jesus Christ, one thing must be made clear, that whilst He walked this earth He was *truly man*. As a man He was tested in every way that we are likely to be, so that as a man He can sympathise with all our weaknesses. He asks nothing of us that He himself has not had to face and so can plead our cause before the throne of God. We might harbour the suspicion that, unlike us, He always had His Deity to fall back on, so that as a 'man' he could never really find himself in the position of an ordinary human being, but this was not so. Consider some of the Gospel records of His life.

We read, "Jesus *grew* in wisdom and stature, and in favour with God and men". Growing physically we can understand, but did the Son of God have to *grow* in wisdom; did He not possess this in its fullness from birth? As a boy of twelve, He asked questions of the teachers in Jerusalem and even as an adult sought answers, which we might have considered He (as God) already knew (Luke

2:52,46). To the disciples He said, "How many loaves do you have?" To the father of a boy possessed by a spirit He asked, "How long has he been like this?" and to Mary, sister of the dead Lazarus He said, "Where have you laid him?" (Mark 6:38; 8:5; 9:21; John 11:34 etc). He even "*learned* obedience from what he suffered" (Hebrews 5:8).

On occasions He expressed surprise and amazement: At the concern of His parents who had returned to Jerusalem to find Him; did they not realise that He had to be in His Father's house? He was surprised at the "lack of faith" of His disciples and amazed when He found the same in those of His hometown. He was "astonished" at the faith of a centurion and seems to have been surprised at the barrenness of a fig tree, and that His disciples were unable to watch with Him in prayer for one hour (Luke 2:49; Mark 4:40; 6:6; Matthew 8:10; Mark 11:13; 14:37).

He exhibited human emotions: He wept over Jerusalem and was "deeply moved in spirit and troubled" when He saw Mary and the Jews with her, weeping at the death of Lazarus, and wept Himself (Luke 19:41; John 11:33-36). The Hebrews' writer tells us, "During the days of Jesus' life on earth, he offered up prayers and petitions with loud cries and tears" (5:7), and weighed down with the thought of the coming trauma, "overwhelmed with sorrow to the point of death", He prayed in Gethsemane, "My Father, if it is possible, may this cup be taken from me. Yet not as I will, but as you will" (Matthew 26:38,39). And as He hung on the cross, He entered into the human experience that prompted the Psalmist to write, "My God, my God, why have you forsaken me?" (Psalm 22:1; Matthew 27:46).

Are we to believe that these very human experiences were just a facade, a pretence put on for the benefit of His disciples and others, or are they proofs of the fact that He is truly man? And none of these aspects of His humanity denies in any way His sinlessness. It is not sinful to not know something, to cry, to exhibit surprise or amazement, to seek, if possible, the removal of a coming trauma or even to feel forsaken. On earth He passed through every human stage of growth; childhood, boyhood to manhood; yet He was "holy, blameless, pure, set apart from sinners" and "tempted in every way, **just as we are**—yet was without sin" (Hebrews 7:26; 4:15).

He is "the image (*eikon*) of the invisible God" (Colossians 1:15), but then 'man' (male and female) was created "in the image (*eikon LXX*) of God" (Genesis 1:27). But it is in Christ—"the second man", that we see 'man' free from all that was inherited from Adam (1 Corinthians 15:47) and realising all that was intended by God when He created man.

Yet Christ on earth frequently showed a 'supernatural' insight: He knew the Samaritan woman had had five husbands: He told Peter where to find a coin (a most unlikely place—a fish) to pay the temple tax, and the disciples where to find the donkey and colt on which He would ride into Jerusalem. He discerned "from the beginning" that Judas would betray him (John 4:17,18; Matthew 17:24-27; 21:1-3; John 6:64) etc. But the miracles He wrought, and His entire ministry and authority, were based on an anointing by the Spirit, in accordance with His own quotation from Isaiah's prophecy:

> The Spirit of the Lord is on me, because he has anointed me to preach good news to the poor. He has sent me to proclaim freedom for the prisoners and recovery of sight for the blind, to release the oppressed ... (Luke 4:18; Isaiah 61:1)

And Peter's comment on this was, "God anointed Jesus of Nazareth with the Holy Spirit and power … he went around doing good and healing ... *because God was with him*" (Acts 10:38). Peter did not say, "*because* he was God". As a man, He did what He did because "God was with him": He said of Himself, "The Son can do nothing by himself; he can do only what he sees his Father doing". At the raising of Lazarus He thanked His Father that He had heard Him and that "you always hear me" (John 5:19; 11:41,42). And His communication in prayer with the Father was characteristic of *human* faith and trust in God, Jesus being the supreme example (see Hebrews 2:9-13). His oneness with the Father in word and action was a direct result of His constant prayers.[4]

In a lesser sense, anointing of the Spirit and speaking the words of God was true also of the prophets of old. Hebrews records, "God spoke to our forefathers through the prophets", and Peter wrote of men who "spoke from God *as they were carried along by the Holy Spirit*" (Hebrews 1:1; 2 Peter 1:21). Christ, *as a man*, was the prophet par excellence; it was His oneness with His Father that enabled Him to do what the Father had sent Him to do, and to do it *as a man* (John 5:36; 6:38; 10:30; 12:49,50 etc). In fact, in respect of the miracles that Christ had been doing, He promised His disciples (mere men), "Anyone who has faith in me will do what I have been doing. He will do even greater things than these, because I am going to the Father" (John 14:11-14).

Whilst there are dispensational aspects attached to the 'miracles' spoken of here (see *The Miracles of the Apostles* M. Penny publ. OBT), it is evident that Jesus was able, even with the limitations of 'man', to do the will of His Father without assuming the prerogatives of Deity. Let us rejoice then in "**the man** Christ Jesus".

# The Christ: An Unfolding Revelation

Nearly 2000 years since the earthly life and ministry of Christ and the Apostles, we look back today with the help of the Scriptures upon all that has been revealed and all that may be known of Jesus Christ. What we now know, with a completed Bible, has not always been known, for that knowledge has been unfolded gradually throughout the ages. From the enigmatic 'promise' overheard by our first parents in Eden, to the revelation of His glory in the New Testament, God's people have come to know more and more of the One Paul described as "the man Christ Jesus". And that revelation has unfolded from the earliest suggestion that He was to come as a human being, to the knowledge that this 'human' is none other than "Immanuel—which means, 'God with us'" (Matthew 1:23); God manifest in the flesh. This unfolding revelation is an unfolding of 'the secret of the Christ (Messiah)'.

# The Secret of The Christ (Messiah)

Paul wrote in Ephesians 3:4,5:

> In reading this, then, you will be able to understand my insight into **the mystery (or secret) of Christ, which was not made known to men in other generations as it has now been revealed** by the Spirit to God's holy apostles and prophets.

There are three aspects of the revelation of God's truth to man resident in these verses. Firstly the timing: He reveals His truth 'in His own good time'. The secret of the Messiah "was not made known ... in other generations *as it has now been revealed*". Remember Ecclesiastes 3:1: "There is a *time* for everything ... under heaven".

Secondly, His revelation of truth is not made known to 'all and sundry'. In Ephesians 3 it is firstly to apostles and prophets and "by the Spirit of God". Similarly, when the Lord hid "the secrets of the kingdom of heaven" in parables, He said to His disciples, "The knowledge of the secrets of the kingdom of heaven *has been given to you (disciples)*, but *not to them (the crowd)*" (Matthew 13:10,11).

Thirdly there is the 'human' element. In Ephesians 3 the secret of the Christ (Messiah) was to "God's *holy* apostles and prophets", and whilst the addition of the word "holy" here may indicate that these men had been specially *set apart* for this revelation, it may also suggest that their way of life, their faithfulness to the Lord— their "holy" life, fitted them for this privilege.

The 'secret of the Christ' has been unfolded gradually throughout the period from Adam to the present dispensation; each stage adding more to our knowledge of Him. In this booklet I can only give a brief outline of some of the 'stages' in that unfolding. One of the difficulties in doing this is to limit our own knowledge of the Christ, to what was understood at the time, so that we do not read into the text what was only revealed at a later stage. A further factor that has to be taken into consideration is that we cannot be sure just how much was understood by those who first wrote or read those things that we today, with the further light of later Scripture, apply to Him. That they may have understood a lot more than we give them credit for is suggested by the Lord Jesus' words to the Jews, "Your father Abraham rejoiced at the thought of *seeing my day; he saw it* and was glad" and when Peter, naming David as a prophet said, "*Seeing what was ahead, he spoke of the resurrection of the Christ*" (John 8:56; Acts 2:29-31see also Galatians 3:8).

So as we journey through the Old Testament we must neither read into it things that belong to a later revelation, nor dismiss the possibility that men of faith might have known more than appears on the surface. Our starting point is a good example of this. Just how much did our first parents know about the Christ? It would seem that Eve might well have thought, quite understandably, that her firstborn son (Cain) was the 'Promised One' who would crush the serpent's head. Later it was to become quite evident that he was not (Genesis 4:1-16; 1 John 3:12).

## The Seed of the Woman:

> The LORD God said to the serpent, "Because you have done this…. I will put enmity between you and the woman, and between your seed and **her seed**; he will crush your head, and you will strike his heel." (Genesis 3:14,15 reading "seed" as the *KJV* instead of the *NIV* "offspring".)

The background to this verse is found in the events that transpired in the Garden of Eden (Genesis 2:7-3:13). The idyllic situation that existed there when the LORD God walked and had fellowship with our first parents had been spoilt. The woman's deception by the serpent (later to be identified as Satan – Revelation 12:9; 20:2) and Adam's disobedience, had let sin into the world, and now all that seemed to await the guilty couple was death. But there was hope, for the judgement of the LORD God upon Adam spoke of "all the days of your **life**", and to Eve He had spoken of her "**offspring**", suggesting the **continuance** of the human race. They had also overheard the judgement pronounced on the serpent—a promised seed, 'the seed of the woman'.

While no New Testament writer quotes Genesis 3:15 as applying to Christ, many commentators from earliest times have seen this as being a reference to the coming Messiah.[5] It has been dubbed the *protevangelium* (the first gospel proclamation). In the light of passages such as Hebrews 2:14 (see also 1 John 3:8) this application seems justified:

> Since the children have flesh and blood, *he too shared in their humanity* so that by his death *he might destroy him who holds the power of death—that is, the devil.*

How much Adam and his wife read into this ancient judgement we cannot say, but it is difficult to see how, in the light of later scriptures, it can apply to any other than Christ. So this may be the first glimmer of light in the revelation of "the man Christ Jesus".

## The Seed of Abraham

Some 2000 years now pass; in terms of biblical chronology, half the history contained in the Old Testament.[6] That history is compressed into eleven chapters of the Old Testament, after which a further revelation of 'the secret of the Messiah' unfolds to Abraham.

> In **your seed** shall all the nations of the earth be blessed (Genesis 22:18, *KJV*)

Although Abraham's "seed" were to be as numerous as "the stars in the sky and as the sand on the seashore" (Genesis 22:17) Paul, quoting this scripture, refers this promise to Christ, **the Seed** of Abraham.

> The promises were spoken to Abraham and to his seed. The Scripture does not say "and to seeds", meaning many

people, but "and to your seed", meaning one person, who is Christ. (Galatians 3:16)

In the above two references we have what is often found in Scripture, a two-fold fulfilment of a prophecy; Abraham's seed *collective* (many people), but also Abraham's Seed *specific* (one Person). In the end event, all the promises of God to Abraham and his seed (plural) are only possible in **the Seed**, Christ Jesus. And it was, of Abraham's seed, "as concerning the flesh (that) Christ came" (Romans 9:4,5 *KJV*).

## The Line of Judah

> The sceptre will not depart from Judah, nor the ruler's staff from between his feet, until **he comes to whom it belongs** and the obedience of the nations is his. (Genesis 49:10)

This prophecy is the specific blessing of Jacob upon his son Judah. The tribe of Judah was to become the royal line in Israel and the Messiah would descend from this tribe. In the New Testament Christ is called "the Lion of the tribe of Judah" (Revelation 5:5 see Hebrews 7:14).

## The Son of David

The Lord said to David, "Your house and your kingdom shall endure for ever before me; your throne shall be established for ever" (2 Samuel 7:16). David became the *standard* by which future kings of Israel were judged (e.g. 2 Kings 16:2; 18:3). And the Lord promised of his seed:

The Lord has sworn to David in truth; He will not turn from it; I will set **one of the fruit of your body** on the throne for you. (Psalm 132:11 lit.)

Partially fulfilled in the nearer context by Solomon, it was expanded in Jewish thinking to refer to the expected Messiah, looked for at the time of the birth of Christ and referred to by Peter on the Day of Pentecost:

David …. being a prophet, and knowing that God swore with an oath to him that **of the fruit of his loins**, as concerning flesh, **to raise the Christ to sit on his throne**, foreseeing he spoke about the resurrection of the Christ. (Acts 2:29-31 lit.)

Messiah was to be David's Son, sit on David's throne and become the King of Israel.

## King of Israel

The monarchy in Israel began as an act of rejection when the elders demanded of Samuel, "appoint a king to lead us, such as all the other nations have". The Lord's reaction was, "they have rejected me as their king"; He, Jehovah was their King. Nevertheless He gave them a king, but warned them that he would turn out to be a tyrant (as he did). So Saul (of the tribe of Benjamin, **not** Judah) became the first king of Israel (1 Samuel 8:4-21). But Saul displeased the Lord and was later rejected by Him. Then the Lord chose David and "the throne of David" was established. After David's death Solomon his son then occupied the throne and then, over a period of some 345 years, it passed down to twenty kings, some good, some bad.[7] But Solomon, in all his glory, never exhausted the Lord's promise on oath to David. That promise awaited fulfilment in the Person of the Messiah.

The kingdom effectively ended, as far as a Jewish king sitting on David's throne was concerned, with the Babylonian captivity and the destruction of Jerusalem and its Temple (circa 586 BC). It was after this period that the promise to David concerning a Coming One to sit on his throne began to crystallise into the Messianic conception held at the time of the birth of Christ; He was expected as 'the King of Israel', who would restore the kingdom to Israel. His birth was foretold to Mary:

> The angel said to her… "You will be with child and give birth to a son, and you are to give him the name **Jesus**…. The Lord God will give him **the throne of his father David**, and **he will reign over the house of Jacob for ever**; his kingdom will never end". (Luke 1:30-33)

The Messiah is identified with "Jesus" who came of the tribe of Judah and "the house of David". But this is to anticipate. When the New Testament opens there is a longing among at least some in Israel for His coming. Simeon was "waiting for the consolation of Israel" and the Holy Spirit had revealed to him "he would not die before he had seen the Lord's Christ" (Luke 2:25,26 cp. also Luke 24:21).

Thirty years later Nathaniel on meeting "this same Jesus", said to Him "Rabbi, you are the Son of God; **you are the king of Israel**" (John 1:49). And just before the Lord's ascension from the Mount of Olives the disciples (having had the things concerning Christ explained to them from the Old Testament Scriptures - Luke 24:25-27,44,45) asked Him the question:

> Lord, are you at this time going **to restore the kingdom to Israel**? (Acts 1:6)

The Messiah had died, had risen again and ascended to heaven; now "He must remain in heaven until the time comes for God **to restore everything**, as he promised long ago through his holy prophets" (Acts 3:21). He was coming back to the Mount of Olives, just as they had seen Him go, to be their king in Jerusalem (Zechariah 14:1-9,16).

## A Prophet like Moses

> The Lord your God will raise up for you **a prophet like me** (like Moses) from among your own brothers. You must listen to him. (Deuteronomy 18:15,18)

At the time Christ was born, the people of Israel were still looking for this prophet, and when John the Baptist began his ministry, having denied he was the Christ, he was asked by the Jews of Jerusalem, "Are you Elijah ... Are you *the Prophet*?" When he answered "No" they said, "Why then do you baptise if you are not the Christ, nor Elijah, nor the Prophet?" (John 1:19-26). Evidently the Jews considered the Messiah and "the Prophet" to be different persons, but Peter speaking shortly after the Day of Pentecost, identifies "the Prophet" with Christ saying:

> Christ ... even Jesus ... must remain in heaven until the time comes for God to restore everything, as he promised long ago through his holy prophets. For Moses said, "The Lord your God will raise up for you *a prophet like me* from among your own people; you must listen to everything he tells you." (Acts 3:20-23)

Moses led Israel out from the slavery in Egypt to the borders of the Promised Land. The Messiah, *a prophet like him*, delivers His people from the slavery of sin and into their 'Promised Land', restoring all that was lost through sin and disobedience, "as (God) promised.... through his holy prophets".

## Messiah: The Anointed One

If the enigmatic 'promise' of Genesis 3:15 does not refer to the promise of the Messiah, since it was never applied by either Old or New Testament writers to Him, then 'the secret of the Messiah' up to this point in time, has been largely concerned with His genealogy.[8] The Seed of Abraham; the line of Judah; the Son of David, the King of Israel. He has also been seen as "the Prophet" promised in the days of Moses, identified much later by Peter as "the Christ" the Messiah.

Up until now I have used the title "Messiah" to refer to the Promised One from the beginning of Scripture, seeing Him as 'the seed of the woman', but the actual Hebrew word *Mashiach* is only translated "Messiah" twice in the Old Testament *KJV* (Daniel 9:25,26) and not at all in the *NIV*, which has "The Anointed One". The word 'Messiah', Greek equivalent 'Christ', derives from the word 'anointed'. Hence Christ is 'The Anointed One'. Anointing in the Old Testament was used to set aside a person for the office of king, priest or prophet (e.g. Saul in 1 Samuel 15:1; Aaron in Exodus 40:13; Elisha in 1 Kings 19:16). Christ holds all these offices; **the Anointed One** par excellence. We have seen Him as "a **Prophet** like Moses" and a **King** to sit on David's throne, and now, as we come to the Psalms, He is revealed as a **Priest** "in the order of Melchizedek". And this introduces the idea of sacrifice in connection with His ministry.

# A Great High Priest

> The Lord has sworn and will not change his mind: "You are a priest for ever, in the order of Melchizedek." (Psalm 110:4)
>
> Jesus ... the Son ... was designated by God to be high priest in the order of Melchizedek ... for ever. (Hebrews 5:6,10; 7:17)

Israel's priesthood derived from Aaron of the tribe of Levi and was to "continue for all generations to come" (Exodus 40:12-15). But the Christ "descended from Judah, and in regard to that tribe Moses said nothing about priests" (Hebrews 7:14).

Christ's priesthood was superior to that from Aaron being "in the order of Melchizedek, not in the order of Aaron". This enigmatic figure who appeared to Abraham and received tithes from him, was "priest of God Most High", king of (Jeru)salem, without any known parents or genealogy and no connection with the failing Levitical priesthood. We know little about Melchizedek's priesthood, apart from the fact that it pre-dated that of Aaron.[9] And unlike Aaron and his descendents whose priesthood was to cease, Christ is "a priest for ever, in the order of Melchizedek" (Hebrews 7:1-25). The writer of Hebrews represents the abiding nature of Melchizedek's priesthood when describing this king-priest as: [10]

> Without father or mother, without genealogy, without beginning of days or end of life, like the Son of God he remains a priest for ever. (7:3)

Melchizedek, the king-priest, and his priesthood, is a type of the priesthood of the Messiah, **the King-Priest**; a priesthood superior to that of Aaron. Compare the differences between the priesthood of Aaron and the priesthood of Melchizedek in Hebrews chapters 7-9:

| Aaron / Levitical | Christ / Order of Melchizedek |
|---|---|
| 1) Many priests, based on *a regulation* as to their ancestry, since death prevented them from continuing. | 1) One priest, based on *an oath*, not related to ancestry; ("without father or mother").[11] An indestructible life. |
| 2) Many sacrifices, "day after day, first for his own sins, and then for the sins of the people". | 2) One sacrifice, once for all, not for His own sins, but for the sins of the people. |
| 3) Unable to make perfect, it was an earthly priesthood, a shadow of the true. | 3) Perfecting the sanctified for ever. The true priesthood associated with heaven itself. |

In the person of the Messiah the offices of both King and High Priest meet; a further step in the unfolding of 'the secret of the Christ'.

## Sacrifice and Offering (Psalm 40)

The revelation of the Messiah as a Priest introduces the idea of sacrifice for, "We do have such a high priest (and) Every high priest is appointed to offer both gifts and sacrifices, and so *it was necessary for this one (Christ) also to have something to offer*" (Hebrews 8:1-3). And what He offered was "himself.... to do away with sin by the sacrifice of himself" (9:24-26).

We are dependent on the New Testament for the above understanding, so I would like to remind readers that we do not know whether those living in Old Testament times related passages in the Psalms and Isaiah (in particular) to the Messiah. Nor do we know if they realised that He must Himself be a sacrifice for sin. Even when we come to the New Testament, Peter, who recognised Jesus as the Messiah, failed to see that He must suffer and die (Matthew 16:13-23). We however, have the added light of the New Testament writers (post-resurrection), and our safest course is to see how they treated these passages.

The risen Christ told His disciples "Everything must be fulfilled that is written about me in the Law of Moses, the Prophets and the Psalms" (Luke 24:44).[12] And there are some 48 references in 16 Psalms relating either directly or indirectly to Him.[13]

> Sacrifice and offering you did not desire.... burnt offerings and sin offerings you did not require. Then I said, "Here I am, I have come—it is written about me in the scroll. I desire to do your will, O my God." (Psalm 40:6-8)

> It is impossible for the blood of bulls and goats to take away sins. *Therefore*, when Christ came into the world, he said: "Sacrifice and offering you did not desire ..... I have come to do your will, O God." (Hebrews 10:4-7)

The Hebrew's writer applies these verses to the Messiah and in his explanation that follows, identifies the will of God with "the sacrifice of the body of Jesus Christ once for all" (vs.9,10). Messiah is the High Priest **and also** the Sacrifice offered. And New Testament writers quoted other Psalms when describing Christ's rejection, crucifixion and resurrection associated with His sacrifice for sin. The following is a selection:

> **His rejection:** "The stone the builders rejected has become the capstone." (Psalm 118:22; Acts 4:11; Matthew 21:42; 1 Peter 2:7 etc)

> **His crucifixion:** "They divide my garments among them and cast lots for my clothing" (22:18; John 19:24). "They gave me vinegar for my thirst" (69:21; John 19:28-30). "He protects all his bones, not one of them will be broken" (34:20; John 19:31-36). And His cry from the cross, "My God, my God, why have you forsaken me?" (22:1; Matthew 27:46)

> **His resurrection:** "You will not abandon me to the grave, nor will you let your Holy One see decay." (16:10; Acts 2:24-27; 13:32-37)

# A Sacrifice for Sin (Isaiah 53)

In the Psalms, apart from the connection in Psalm 40 between the sacrifice of animals, which any Jew would associate with cleansing from sin, and its antitype, the 'coming' of the Messiah to do the will of God and to be **the** Sacrifice for sin, there is little (if any) to suggest that the *reason* for the 'sacrifice' of the Messiah was related to the forgiveness of sins.

Sacrifices and offerings are spoken of from the very beginning (Cain and Abel Genesis 4; Hebrews 11:4) and with hindsight we see that Abraham's offering of Isaac, *his only son*, set forth symbolically the sacrifice of God's only Son, Christ. Also the levitical system of sacrifices pointed forward in type and shadow to the vital truth; "without the shedding of blood there is no forgiveness (of sins)" (Hebrews 9:22). But it is not until we come to the words of Isaiah that we get anything like a *clear* conception in the Old Testament of the connection between **His** sacrifice and **His people's sin**; look at chapter 53 in particular[14].

> **HE WAS** pierced **for our** transgressions, **HE WAS** crushed **for our** iniquities; the punishment **that brought us** peace **WAS UPON HIM**, and **BY HIS** wounds **we are** healed … the LORD has **LAID ON HIM** the iniquity **of us all** etc. (Isaiah 53:5-12)

Keeping this in context "our" in these verses applied initially to Judah and Jerusalem (1:1). In the wider context this sacrifice for sin is seen as embracing Israel (Acts 5:31) and then the Gentiles (Acts 11:18; 13:38,39,46-48). This aspect of the revelation of 'the secret of the Christ' is set forth in type in the Old Testament sacrifices, hidden in enigmatic language, but without the light of the New Testament, apparently not clearly grasped by even God's people. The New Testament identifies this Messiah, pierced and crushed for our iniquities, with Jesus of Nazareth.

## Born of a Virgin (Isaiah 7)

In the days of Ahaz, king of Judah (circa 730 B.C.) the prophet Isaiah, speaking for the Lord, gave the king a 'sign'; a sign that some 700 years later was applied to Jesus of Nazareth.

| To Ahaz | To Joseph |
|---------|-----------|
| The Lord himself will give you a sign: The virgin will be with child and will give birth to a son, and will call him Immanuel. (Isaiah 7:14) | (Mary) will give birth to a Son, and you are to give him the name Jesus, because he will save his people from their sins. All this took place to fulfil what the Lord had said through the prophet: "The virgin will be with child and will give birth to a son, and they will call him Immanuel"—which means "God with us". (Matthew 1:21-23) |

For our purposes, the relevance of this 'promise' as a "sign" to Ahaz does not concern us; its application to Jesus, the Messiah, does.[15] For the moment, and since we are at present considering the human side of the Messiah, we note that He was "born of a virgin". What are the implications of this?

The initial 'promise' concerning the Messiah was that He would be 'the seed of **the woman**', not the seed of the man. Whilst the "seed" of the man has been involved in the birth of every human being to date (bar Eve), it was deliberately, and necessarily avoided in the begetting of the Messiah:

> Joseph son of David, do not be afraid to take Mary home as your wife, because *what is conceived in her is from the Holy Spirit* … You are to give him the name Jesus. (Matthew 1:20,21; see Luke 1:34,35)

In Luke 1:35 the one named "Jesus" is called "the holy one" and we are reminded many times in the New Testament that He was sinless (e.g. 2 Corinthians 5:21; Hebrews 4:15; 7:26; 1 Peter 1:19; 2:21,22; 1 John 3:5). In 1 Peter 2:22, it is noteworthy that the Apostle refers his readers to Isaiah 53:9 in demonstration of His sinlessness, "He committed no sin, and no deceit was found in his mouth".[16] Hence His sinlessness was foreseen in the Old Testament. This sinlessness was vital to our salvation, both in the means of Christ's birth and throughout every moment of His life as a 'man'. Whilst He was "tempted in every way, just as we are", He was "yet without sin" (Hebrews 4:15). Likewise, He must never have inherited, as is the lot of every other human being, what has been passed down to us by Adam: "Sin entered the world through one man, and death through sin, and in this way death came to all men, because all sinned" (Romans 5:12).[17]

Much has been written on how Jesus could be "born of a woman" (Galatians 4:4) and not be a partaker in man's sin. A lot of it is speculation and we may never know the whole truth in this life. It is evident from the Scriptures however, that 'woman' is not sinless, whether it be Eve, Mary or any other woman (Romans 3:23), but the Scriptures also make it clear that Adam, who was given one prohibition in the Garden of Eden *before* the LORD God "made a woman" (Genesis 2:16,17,20-22) is held responsible for the entrance of sin into the world; the woman was deceived, he was not (Genesis 3:13; cp.1 Timothy 2:14). Hence the Messiah must not be identified with Adam's "seed" or be a partaker in the sin he has passed down to the race of men. He must **not** have a human father.

We may never understand the virgin birth (or as some would have it, "virginal conception" *New Bible Dictionary*) except in the terms in which it is set out in the opening chapters of the Gospels of Matthew and Luke. But it is evident that if the Messiah was to be free from sin, that must include *the manner* of His conception. And to be born of a virgin was an outward "sign" (Isaiah 7:14 above) that he had not been conceived by a human father.

## The Man Christ Jesus: A Summary

Our knowledge of Christ Jesus as a 'man' has been an unfolding revelation. From the first hint that He would be 'the seed of the woman', the Scriptures reveal His genealogy through the patriarch Abraham, the royal line of Judah to king David, upon whose throne He was to sit as king of Israel. Combined in His person also was the office of High-priest, but not after the order of the Levitical priesthood which began with Aaron, but after the order of a priesthood that pre-dated it—that of Melchizedek, an enigmatic figure that set forth in type both an endless life and a permanent priesthood. The third in His trio of offices was to be a prophet like Moses. These offices were conveyed by anointing, so He was "**the** Anointed One"—The Messiah, The Christ.

Just as the many high priests in the Old Testament who entered the Holy of Holies once a year with their sacrifices, but who were unable to continue through death, so He, as High-priest, must necessarily have a sacrifice to bring to God. He offered Himself as **the** sacrifice for sins, once for all and "has a permanent priesthood" (Hebrews 7:24). As that sacrifice He must Himself be free from sin and so must be uncontaminated with the "seed" of man. Hence the manner of His birth, "born of a woman" without a biological human father, the outward "sign" of which was His virginal conception.

But now, having been concerned with the human side of the Messiah's nature, we arrive, through the same promise and fulfilment of Isaiah 7:14, to His other side: "call him Immanuel" (which means "God with us" – Matthew 1:23).

# Part 2:
# God With Us

# Part 2:
# God With Us

In tracing the revelation of 'the secret of the Christ' so far in the Old Testament, through His genealogy and the offices He holds as prophet, priest and king, there has been little, if any reason to see Him as any other than "the man Christ Jesus". True, a man above all other men, but a man nevertheless. It is when we reach the Psalms that the Old Testament Scriptures begin to reveal that other side to His nature—His Deity. And it is not until Isaiah's prophecy referred to above, that we get the definite statement that leads us to see Him as "God with us".

## David's Son – David's Lord (Psalm 110)

Psalm 110 is the Psalm of the King–Priest and one of the most quoted or alluded to Psalms in the New Testament.[18] Jesus himself referred to it during His earthly ministry, leaving the opening words for the Pharisees to mull over. They must have known the passage He was referring to in the original Hebrew, and the implications of His question to them would be plain.

> While the Pharisees were gathered together, Jesus asked them, "What do you think about the Christ? Whose son is he?" "The son of David" they replied. He said to them, "How is it then that David, speaking by the Spirit, calls him 'Lord'? For he says, 'The Lord said to my Lord: Sit at my right hand until I put your enemies under your feet'. If then David calls him 'Lord', how can he be his son?" No-one could say a word in reply. (Matthew 22:41-45)

Jesus endorsed this Psalm as "of David" speaking "by the Spirit", when calling the Messiah (Christ) "Lord". The Old Testament Passage He quoted from reads:

> The LORD (*Jehovah*) says to my Lord (*Adonai*): Sit at my right hand until I make your enemies a footstool for your feet. (Psalm 110:1)

*Jehovah* (LORD) was **the Name** by which God made himself known to Israel (Exodus 3:13-15). *The Companion Bible* (Appendix 4) gives its meaning as "*The Eternal* ... He who WAS, and IS, and IS TO COME" and refers to Genesis 21:33 for its definition: "Abraham ... called upon the name of the LORD (*Jehovah*), the **everlasting God**". Moffatt, in his translation, renders *Jehovah*, "The Eternal".

It is a pity that *a name*, JEHOVAH, has been translated in most English versions of the Bible by *a title* – "LORD".[19] Dr. E.W. Bullinger observed, "Jehovah is a proper name, and should be no more translated 'LORD' than Samuel should be translated 'Heard'; or Gershom, 'Stranger'; or Ephraim, 'Fruitful' etc".[20]

To appreciate what is said of the Messiah in this Psalm, I give a brief structure of its seven verses, demonstrating the different use of "LORD" (*Jehovah*) and "Lord" (*Adonai*) in the original Hebrew. In the first half of the Psalm we see Messiah as King; in the second as Priest.

A    **Jehovah** says to my **Adonai**: Sit at my right hand until I
(**Jehovah**) make your enemies a footstool
  B    **Jehovah** will extend your (**Adonai's**) mighty sceptre from
Zion….you (**Adonai**) will rule
    C    Your enemies….your troops
      D    Refreshment….the dew of your youth
A    **Jehovah** has sworn….You (**Adonai**) are a priest for ever in
the order of Melchizedek
  B    **Adonai** is at your (**Jehovah's**) right hand…. (**Adonai**) will
crush kings and judge nations
    C    Nations….rulers
      D    Refreshment….a brook beside the way

Note how Jehovah and Messiah are completely at one. Jehovah makes the Messiah's enemies a footstool and extends His (Messiah's) reign; Messiah crushes kings and rulers and judges nations. The same Messiah, His priestly *sacrificial* work complete, sits down at Jehovah's right hand. The battle and triumph in this conflict are only interrupted by the Messiah's pause to renew His strength (the dew) and the final rest after the battle is won (a brook beside the way).

The first line of the Psalm begins literally (in the Hebrew text): "Of David a Psalm. A statement (or oracle) of Jehovah to my Lord." [21] So what was the "oracle" of Jehovah to David's Lord? It begins:

> Sit at my right hand until I make your enemies a footstool
> for your feet. (110:1)

## The Exalted Messiah

The authority and power of the Messiah spoken of in Psalm 110, go beyond anything that can be true of an earthly king, sitting on the earthly throne of David. However, we need the New Testament to do complete justice to the words of this Psalm.[22] But David's words now reveal another aspect of 'the secret of the Christ'—His exaltation to the right hand of God. Peter's use of this Psalm on the Day of Pentecost, confirms that the exaltation spoken of the Messiah is fulfilled in "this same Jesus":

> David did not ascend to heaven, and yet he said, "The Lord said to my Lord: 'Sit at my right hand until I make your enemies a footstool for your feet'". Therefore let all Israel be assured of this: God has made **this Jesus**, whom you crucified, both Lord and Christ. (Acts 2:34-36)

David's "Lord" was to sit at the right hand of *Jehovah*, His enemies as His footstool. Paul later refers these words to Christ, the Son of God, as he looks forward to that future day when "God is all in all":

> Then the end will come, when he (Christ the Son) hands over the kingdom to God the Father *after he has destroyed all dominion, authority and power. For he must reign until he has put all his enemies under his feet* … When he has done this, then the Son himself will be made subject to him who put everything under him, so that God may be all in all. (1 Corinthians 15:24-28)

Here we anticipate the Father–Son relationship assumed by God to bring the purpose of the ages to fruition; a goal not attained until every enemy of that purpose is destroyed, including death itself.

The remaining verses in the Psalm 110 illustrate the authority and power given to the exalted Messiah at the right hand of God. The use of this Psalm (together with Psalm 16) in the New Testament applies these words to Jesus of Nazareth, the Messiah:

After the Lord Jesus had spoken to them, he was taken up into heaven and *he sat at the right hand of God*. (Mark 16:19)

"God has raised this Jesus to life, and we are all witnesses to the fact. *Exalted to the right hand of God*, he has…. poured out what you now see and hear. For David said, 'the Lord said to my Lord "Sit at my right hand …"'" (Acts 2:32-35)

Christ Jesus who died—more than that, who was raised to life – *is at the right hand of God* and is also interceding for us. (Romans 8:34)

That power…. which he exerted in Christ when he raised him from the dead and *seated him at his right hand* in the heavenly realms. (Ephesians 1:19,20)

And many more references

Mark, Peter and Paul apply the words of Psalm 110 to Jesus the Messiah. That Psalm refers to a King who will rule in the midst of His enemies, crushing kings and judging nations, and a Priest for ever. These words could not be fulfilled in David, Solomon or any other seed of man.

## LORD and Messiah in the Septuagint (*LXX*)

Before we leave the Old Testament revelation of the Messiah as Lord, note how the translators of the Old Testament into Greek (loosely referred to as 'The Septuagint' or *LXX*) handled the word *Jehovah*. This version cannot take preference over the Hebrew text but is a useful 'bridge' between the Old and New Testaments, as the New Testament writers often quoted from it. This is especially so in Hebrews (which emphasises Christ as Lord and High-priest) where "The text of the quotations (from the O.T.) agrees in the main with some form of the present text of the *LXX*" (B.F. Westcott). The translators of the *LXX* were faced with the problem of rendering the sacred name *Jehovah* into Greek and **they regularly chose the title *kurios* ("Lord")** for their purpose.[23]

*Kurios* does service for an ascending series of meanings in the New Testament, from the polite address "Sir" (John 12:21), "owner" (Luke 19:33), "masters" (Matthew 6:24) to "Lord" used of Christ Himself (John 1:23 etc). Quite early in His ministry, Jesus assumed the title "Lord" in the higher sense of Himself, when He said, "Not everyone who says to me, '*Lord, Lord*', will enter the kingdom of heaven, but only he who does the will of *my Father*" (Matthew 7:21). But although some of Jesus' disciples recognised Him as the Messiah before His resurrection (Andrew in John 1:41; Peter in Matthew 16:16 margin), the revelation of Him as "Lord" in the higher sense did not become clear to them until after He had risen from the dead. It was only then that Thomas confessed Him as "My Lord (*Kurios*) *and* my God" (John 20:28). W.E. Vine noted in his *Expository Dictionary* that after this confession (apart from Acts 10:3,4 and Revelation 7:13,14):

> There is no record that *kurios* was ever again used by believers in addressing any save God and the Lord Jesus; cp. Acts 2:47 with 4:29,30 ("Lord" *in loco*).

It seems to have become increasingly obvious to the disciples that the JEHOVAH of the Old Testament was manifest in the JESUS of the New. And the use of *Kurios* when referring to Jesus by the

New Testament writers (knowing that it was used by the *LXX* to translate the Hebrew *Jehovah*) confirms this.

## You are My Son (Psalm 2)

Psalm 2 is quoted or alluded to in Revelation a number of times, where the mysterious and symbolic language used there, describe the ultimate triumph of the glorified Christ in the imagery of the Psalm. In Revelation 1:5 Jesus Christ, the one who "is coming with the clouds" (v.7) is seen as "the ruler of the kings of the earth"; in 2:26,27 He offers the overcomer "authority over the nations" to "rule them with an iron sceptre"; in 19:15 as the Word of God He is again said to "strike down the nations (and) rule them with an iron sceptre". These are allusions to Psalm 2:7-9 where this triumph refers to "my Son" who will have the nations for His inheritance, and "will rule them with an iron sceptre".

Peter and John ascribe this Psalm to David speaking "by the Holy Spirit" in Acts 4:23-26, and again make the connection between "Jesus" and The Messiah (the Anointed One). In this Psalm we have a further revelation of the Anointed One, as "my Son" (v.7):

> I will proclaim the decree of the LORD (*Jehovah*): He said to me, "You are my Son; today I have become your Father." (*NIV*)

> I will declare the decree: the LORD hath said to me "Thou art my Son; this day have I begotten thee." (*KJV*)

A fuller revelation of the Father–Son manifestation of God awaits the New Testament, especially John's Gospel, but here we have the first hint of it in the words of David: Messiah is God's "Son". Just how much David understood of this connection is impossible to say (again it is difficult to put to one side what we know later from the New Testament), but to say that this knowledge is too advanced for one who lived a thousand years before Christ, is to assume too much. David was a prophet (Acts 2:29,30). Like Abraham, who lived some thousand years earlier and who saw and rejoiced in the Messiah's day, David "spoke of the resurrection of the Christ" (John 8:56; Acts 2:29-31). Why should he not have seen the Messiah as God's Son?[24]

## Son of God: Begotten Today

Whether we read Psalm 2:7 in the *KJV* or the *NIV* we are confronted with 'a point in time': "**This day** have I **begotten** thee" or "**today** I have **become** your Father". At what 'point in time' then was the Son "begotten"? Does this detract from His Deity? We need the New Testament (Hebrews 1:1-9) to really show that these words apply to the Messiah ("His Anointed One" Psalm.2: 2) and that they reach beyond any application they may have had to either David or Solomon. Hebrews uses many quotations from the Psalms to demonstrate the superiority of the Son of God.[25] In chapter 2:5-10 the writer identifies "the Son" with Jesus.

In approaching the Father-Son relationship, the words of B.F. Westcott are worthy of note: "The divine being of the Son can be represented to men **only under human figures** (my emphasis)".[26] If language is to make any sense at all (and language is all we have at present in trying to understand the things of God) then we should remind ourselves that there is no such thing as 'a son' without there being, or having been, 'a father' and vice versa. Also that 'a father' and his firstborn 'son' are designated as such, *at the same point in time*. So the titles 'Father' and 'Son' are relative and simultaneous. The 'invisible' God, for the purpose of Creation and Redemption, has *assumed* the 'Persons' (see Appendix 2) of 'Father' and 'Son'.

And this does not detract from the Deity of Christ whatever conclusions we draw about the 'begetting' of the Son, the Father–Son relationship belongs to **the same point in time**.

Jesus is named as "the Son of God" at the annunciation of His birth, at His baptism, transfiguration, crucifixion and resurrection:

> The holy one to be **born** will be called **the Son of God**. (Luke 1:35)

> As soon as Jesus was **baptised**…. a voice from heaven said, "This is **my Son**, whom I love; with him I am well pleased." (Matthew 3:16,17)

> Jesus was **transfigured** before them…. a voice from the cloud said, "This is **my Son**, whom I love; with him I am well pleased." (Matthew 17:1-5)

> They **crucified** him….the centurion and those with him who were guarding Jesus….exclaimed, "Surely he was **the Son of God**!" (Matthew 27:35,54)

> Christ Jesus….declared with power to be **the Son of God**, by his **resurrection** from the dead. (Romans 1:1,4)

In addition to this He is recognised and confessed as such by John the Baptist, Nathaniel, Peter and other of the disciples, as well as demons and evil spirits. He also acknowledged Himself as "the Son of God" before the chief priests and teachers of the law.[27] But when was this Father-Son relationship assumed by God?

At first sight the *KJV* rendering of Psalm 2:7, "Thou art my Son; *this day have I begotten thee*" might seem to teach, the relationship began 'at His birth'. But we are told that God "**sent**" His Son into the world (John 3:17; Galatians 4:4) and this may suggest that *the relationship* pre-dates His manifestation in the flesh. For a son to be "sent" somewhere presupposes that he is already a son. So He was sent from God, already "the Son of God", into this world, which He entered as a babe. Also, as a "Son",

He prayed to His "Father", "Now, Father, glorify me in your presence with the glory **I had with you before the world began**" (John 17:5). And again the writer to the Hebrews, speaking of "His (God's) Son" says of Him, "whom he appointed heir of all things, and through whom he made the universe (lit.'ages')" (Hebrews 1:2).

F.F. Bruce (*in loco*) says of the use of the word *aiones* (lit. 'ages') here, "The whole created universe of space and time is meant, and the affirmation that God brought this universe into being by the agency of His Son is in line with the statements of other New Testament writers that 'all things were made through him; and without him was not anything made that has been made' (John 1:3) and that 'all things have been created through him, and unto him' (Colossians 1:16)". And as William L. Lane remarks in *Word Biblical Commentary* on this verse in Hebrews, "Since Jesus was the one through whom God created the world, he must be the pre-existent Son of God".

Whatever, and whenever, "this day" or "today" refers to in Psalm 2:7, it seems to indicate some point in time (as we understand time) when the Father-Son relationship began and that appears to pre-date not only Christ's birth at Bethlehem, but the creation of the universe.

# The Messiah (the Son) as God (Psalm 45)

> **Touching the king** ... Thy throne, O God, is for ever and ever: the sceptre of thy kingdom is a right sceptre. (Psalm 45:1,6 *KJV*)[28]

> **About the Son** he says, "Your throne, O God, will last for ever and ever, and righteousness will be the sceptre of your kingdom." (Hebrews 1:8 *NIV*)

Such words could never be exhausted in either David or Solomon, and the Hebrews' writer confirms this and applies them to Jesus, the Messiah, "the Son of God". Taken together with the later words of Isaiah, they leave no doubt concerning the Deity of the Son:

> To us a child is born, to us a son is given, and the government will be on his shoulders. And he will be called Wonderful Counsellor, **Mighty God**, Everlasting Father, Prince of Peace. Of the increase of his government and peace there will be no end. (9:6,7; cp. Jeremiah 23:5,6)

"Mighty God" is *El Gibbor* in the Hebrew, used as a designation of God Himself in such passages as Isaiah 10:21 and Jeremiah 32:18. In Isaiah 9:6 it is applied to one whose birth is promised to the people of Israel and alluded to in Luke 2:10,11 where it refers to Jesus. His birth will bring great joy "for all the (lit.) people"; a Saviour born in the city of David; "He is Christ the Lord".

# Through Him All Things Were Made (Psalm 102)

I have already touched upon the fact that God created the universe through the agency of "His Son" (Hebrews 1:2). The writer of Hebrews also quotes Psalm 102:25-27, that attributes the creation of heaven and earth to "my God (Hebrew *El* v.24)", to show that this work of creation was the work of the Son.

He used the Greek version of Psalm 102 (101 in that version) when quoting verse 25, which adds the vocative "O Lord (*Kurie*)", in applying this passage to the Son. And readers will remember that this version regularly uses *Kurios* when translating God's Old Testament name of *Jehovah*. Further, in verse 27 of the Psalm we read, "You *remain the same*, and your years will *never end*"; quoted in Hebrews 1:12 and alluded to later (13:8), "Jesus Christ *is the same* yesterday and today and *forever*". The three versions read as follows:

> **Hebrew O.T:** O my God (*El*)… In the beginning you laid the foundations of the earth, and the heavens are the work of your hands … (Psalm 102:24-27)

> **Greek OT:** In the beginning thou, O Lord (*Kurie*), didst lay the foundation of the earth; and the heavens are the works of thine hands … (Psalm 102:25-27 *LXX*)

> **Greek N.T:** About the Son…. He also says, "In the beginning, O Lord (*Kurie*), you laid the foundations of the earth, and the heavens are the work of your hands …" (Hebrews 1:8,10-12)

The Hebrews' writer in quoting this Psalm and relating it to the Son later identifies Him as 'Jesus' (2:5-9), agreeing with what both Paul and John say of the Messiah confirming that, "the Old Testament Creator is the Son of God who acted as the Father's agent in creation. He may, therefore, in keeping with the author's insight, view the one described throughout the Old Testament as the Creator and Sustainer of all things as also the one who was to come as Messiah".[29]

> **Paul:** The Son he loves … By him all things were created: things in heaven and on earth, visible and invisible, whether thrones or powers or rulers or authorities; all things were created by him and for him. He is before all things, and in him all things hold together. (Colossians 1:13-17)

> **John:** The Word … Through him all things were made; without him nothing was made that has been made … The Word became flesh. (John 1:1-3, 10,11,14)

> **The writer of Hebrews:** His Son, whom he appointed heir of all things, and through whom he made the universe. (Hebrews 1:2)

# Part 3:
# God Manifest
# in the Flesh

# Part 3: God Manifest in the Flesh[30]

In the first two parts of this booklet I have considered the two aspects of Jesus as God and man. These I have as far as possible kept apart for the purposes of understanding, but never, I hope, have I lost sight of the fact that they are so intertwined that the one cannot be really understood apart from the other. It is when we come to the New Testament that this dual aspect of the Messiah becomes clearer, but before we leave the Old it would be wrong not to look at Isaiah's prophecy again, to see that in the very name given to the Messiah, He was "God with us". Named as "Immanuel" we see Him as God *manifest* in the flesh.

## Immanuel: God With Us

Isaiah said to Ahaz, king of Judah:

> The Lord himself will give you a sign: The virgin will be with child and will give birth to a son, and will call him **Immanuel**. (Isaiah 7:14)

And Matthew (1:21- 23) records of the birth of the Messiah:

> You are to give him the name Jesus, because he will save his people from their sins. All this took place to fulfil what the Lord had said through the prophet: "The virgin will be

with child and will give birth to a son, and they will call him **Immanuel**"—which means "God **with us**".

The only other occurrences of this name are in Isaiah 8:8 ("Immanuel") and 8:10 ("God is with us") used in the immediate context of the threat of Assyria as the Lord's instrument of judgement on Judah in the days of Isaiah. But in the New Testament, there is no record after Matthew 1:23 that Jesus was ever called Immanuel, although in the framework of Matthew's Gospel the name (God with us) in this verse is balanced by the closing words of the Gospel, "Jesus said ... 'Surely I am **with you** always, to the very end of the age'" (28:18-20). Also He promised, "Where two or three come together in my name, there am I **with them**" (18:20).

"Immanuel" is the assurance of the Lord's presence *with His people* and although Joseph was instructed by the angel to call Mary's child "Jesus" (vs. 20,21), the promise that "**they** (third person plural) will call him Immanuel" is prophetic of a future day when 'all Israel' recognise the presence of the Lord **with them**, a fact that was not true of His first coming, but will be when He returns to them (Zechariah 12:10-14; 14:4-9; Matthew 24:30,31; Acts 1:6-11; Revelation 1:7 etc). The presence of Jesus with His people is the fulfilment of the promise "God with us" (Immanuel).

The Psalmist expressed the assurance of the **presence** of God among His people when he wrote of "the city of God, the holy place where the Most High dwells":

> God is within her, she will not fall ... The LORD Almighty (Jehovah of Hosts) **is with us** ... The LORD Almighty **is with us.** (46:4-7, 11)

This Psalm, which gives the assurance of the presence of Jehovah, "an ever present help in trouble" (v.1) was "a celebration of the security of Jerusalem" and "it remained for Israel a song of hope celebrating the certain triumph of God's kingdom" (*NIV* Study Bible *in loco*). It promises God's protection and presence in natural (vs.2,3) and international (v.6) catastrophes. And it will only be fulfilled in its fullness when the Lord returns to His people as Immanuel. And He will be "this same Jesus".

## His voluntary humility (Philippians 2:5-8)

There is no passage of Scripture that reveals 'the secret of the Christ' from His exalted position in time past, through His voluntary humiliation, to His exaltation to the highest place, like Philippians 2:5-11. And yet the main reason Paul wrote these words was to draw attention to the "attitude" of Christ Jesus (v.5) using it as an example for the Philippian believers to follow. He did not (initially at least) write these words to prove either the Deity of Christ or that He is truly man. We can however, rejoice at the light it throws on *Jesus: God and Man* and be thankful for the "mind that was in Christ Jesus" that resulted in our salvation. Philippians 2:5-8 (*KJV*):

---

Let this mind be in you, which was also in Christ Jesus:

Who, being in the form of God, thought it not robbery to be equal with God:

But made himself of no reputation, and took upon him the form of a servant,

and was made in the likeness of men:

And being found in fashion as a man, he humbled himself,

and became obedient unto death, even the death of the cross (*KJV*)

---

Volumes have been written on this passage and every key word is worthy of serious study; a task that is too great for a small booklet.[31] I have therefore confined myself to touching on those questions most relevant to our subject; 'What did Paul mean by "the form of God" and "the form of a servant"', and did Christ Jesus *exchange* the one for the other? Consider first the context in which the passage is set:

> Look not every man on his own things, but every man also on the things of others. Let this mind be in you.... (vs.3,4)

As noted already, Paul did not initially write this epistle to teach the doctrine of the Deity of Christ, but uses the "mind" that was in Christ Jesus in this passage as an **example**. He considered "the interests of others" and put them before His own. In 2 Corinthians 8:9 Paul summed it up succinctly when he wrote, "For you know the grace of our Lord Jesus Christ, that though he was rich, yet for your sakes he became poor, so that you through his poverty might become rich".

In the passage before us this is seen in that though "being in the form (*morphe*) of God", He voluntarily took "the form (*morphe*) of a servant (lit.slave)".

The *NIV* rendering of *morphe* as "very nature" does, I believe, better express (in modern parlance) what the Apostle meant (and this should come out in what follows). But this is an interpretation rather than a translation, and most of the commentators I have consulted have preferred the *KJV* "form" as a rendering of the word[32]. Since I will be quoting some of them I will do likewise.

# Form (*morphe*) and Appearance (*schema*)

**Schema:** It is evident from the Gospel records that Jesus *looked* much like any other man. He was "made in human likeness" (v.7 *NIV*). We do not know whether His clothes distinguished Him from other men so that he would be recognised as a servant (and we must remember that the word translated "servant" (*doulos*) meant literally a "slave") but I believe it is unlikely. If He did dress differently, it is more likely that it was as a Rabbi (John 1:38,49) although it was probably the authority with which He spoke that led men like Andrew and Nathaniel to call Him such (cp. Matthew 7:28,29). Jesus' appearance (*schema*) referred to His *outward* appearance; He was much like other men.

**Morphe:** It is of course quite possible that outward appearance does not always convey what a person really is, hence we have sayings such as, "he is not what he seems to be" and recall the Lord's warning concerning "wolves in sheep's clothing". Also, "you cannot judge a book by its cover". This is where the difference between "appearance" (*schema*) and "form" (*morphe*) begins to become clearer. So what then do the phrases mean that speak of Christ Jesus as "being in the form (*morphe*) God" and taking "the form (*morphe*) of a servant"? What is the form of God; what is the form of a servant?

The Greek word *morphe* occurs only three times in the New Testament (twice in the above passage). The first and only other reference to it is in Mark 16:12 which shows that it must *include* within its meaning the idea of outward form. "Afterwards Jesus appeared (lit. was revealed) in a different *form* to two of them while they were walking in the country". I say include, because this does not exhaust its meaning. In Philippians 2:6,7 it is seen in contrast to *schema* (appearance v.8). Christ Jesus was "in *appearance* as a man" but took "the *form* of a servant".

Here are four definitions of *morphe* culled from the Dictionaries and Commentaries I have consulted on the word *morphe*. They represent the views of early and late 20th century expositors:

> *Morphe* always signifies a form which truly and fully expresses the being which underlies it. (*Vocabulary of the Greek New Testament* Moulton and Milligan).

> It can mean the embodiment of the form.... The outward appearance cannot be detached from the essence of the thing; the essence of the thing is indicated by its outward form. (*NIV Theological Dictionary of New Testament Words*).

> The 'form of God' is the sum of the characteristics which make the being we call 'God', specifically God, rather than some other being—an angel, say. (*The Person and Work of Christ* p. 39 B.B. Warfield).

> I must conclude that the weight of linguistic evidence is still on the side of J. B. Lightfoot who demonstrated from a study of both its usage throughout the history of Greek thought and the occurrences of the *morph-* root in the New Testament that *morphe* refers to the 'essential attributes' of a thing. (*Jesus Divine Messiah* pp. 448,449 Robert L. Reymond). [33]

These scholars and others concur largely that "the *form* of God" refers to "His essential attributes" and is reflected in the way He represents Himself outwardly. In Christ Jesus we *see* something of

God's essential nature in the way He acted, spoke etc—"In Christ all the fullness of the Deity (Godhead) lives in bodily form" (Colossians 2:9).

So also the "*form* of a servant" must likewise refer to "the essential nature" that makes a person we call "a servant", a servant. Hence the *NIV* rendering "very nature" seems a good *interpretation* of the original both in respect of God and servant. The word rendered "servant" is the Greek *doulos* in the Philippians passage, a word used many times in the New Testament and having several nuances. At one end of the scale it can mean a slave (Colossians 3:11; Philemon 15,16), who in Greek contemporary society was considered of a contemptible lower class, at the other a trusted "servant" (Matthew 24:45). But in all cases the requirement of a *doulos* was 'obedience' (Ephesians 6:5; Colossians 3:22; 1 Timothy 6:1). When Christ Jesus took the "form of a *doulos*" His ultimate obedience was "obedience unto death" (Philippians 2:8).

## Made Himself Nothing (*kenosis*)

When Christ Jesus, "being in the form of God" took "the form of a servant", did He *exchange* the one "nature" for the other? Did He empty Himself of His Deity? The idea that Christ Jesus "emptied Himself" comes from a literal interpretation of the Greek verb *kenoo* and *The Revised Version* actually translates the word in this way. Other versions avoid this rendering; the *KJV* has "made of no reputation" and the *NIV* "made nothing". If we insist on the rendering, "he emptied himself", we are immediately stuck with the question, 'of what did He empty Himself?' And various answers have been given to this—'His glory' is a popular one. Rather than pursuing this question, I would rather interpret the meaning of *kenoo* from what we have already discovered about Christ Jesus when He was "made in the likeness of men".

Look back to what was said under the heading, 'Jesus: Truly Man' and recall the total dependence He, as the Son of God, had on His Father (John 5:19). I cannot repeat it all here, but let R. A. Finlayson sum it up: "In this voluntary self-emptying, Christ relinquished His hold on the resources of Deity, and these were ministered to Him constantly by the Holy Spirit as He needed them for His task".[34] Put this together with Paul's words in Colossians 2: 9 (see also 1:19), "In Christ all the fullness of the Deity (Godhead) **lives in bodily form**", and we see that He never relinquished Deity, only *the resources* of Deity, and, in common with the dependence of His disciples, He only called upon those resources for the purposes of fulfilling His ministry. He said of Himself, "By myself I can do nothing"; He made Himself totally dependent on His Father—He never fell back on His Deity. To do so would give the lie to His being truly man with all the weakness and dependence that involved.

The nearest I can get to an example from life is of a king who sends his son, the prince, into the army. He says to the commanding officer, "my son is to get no privileges; he is to be treated like any other recruit, and in any recourse to you, his case is to be treated the same as any other". In this example, the prince *never ceases at any time* to be a prince, but he does relinquish the privileges attached to his position.

## The Name above Every Name (Philippians 2:9-11)

The second part of this wonderful passage outlining the example of Christ, hinges on the word, "Therefore" (*dio*), because of this. Because He humbled Himself, even to enduring "death on a cross! **Therefore** God exalted him to the highest place". Recalling that this passage was originally written to encourage believers to have the *mind* that was in Christ Jesus, Paul reminds them that in the divine order, self-humbling inevitably leads to exaltation, seen in its fullness in the example of Christ, but equally applicable to the Philippians. Compare Matthew 18:4, "Whoever humbles himself like this child is the greatest in the kingdom of heaven".

Christ's exaltation to the highest place is not revealed here for the first time; we have seen it already in the Old Testament (Psalm 110:1 quoted in Hebrews 1:13) but here in Philippians is added:

> And gave him the name that is above every name, that at the name of Jesus every knee should bow, in heaven and on earth and under the earth, and every tongue confess that Jesus Christ is Lord, to the glory of God the Father.

So what is "the name that is above every name"? Some say 'Jesus', reading, "that *at the name Jesus* every knee should bow". I would have no problem with 'bowing the knee' to that name, but I feel that in view of what follows, "every tongue confess that Jesus Christ is **Lord**", it is more likely to be *Jehovah* (as a name, ***not*** a title). This was God's sacred name amongst the Jews, a name they forbore to speak. I have already observed that it is a pity that the Hebrew *Jehovah* has been rendered 'LORD' in most English Bibles, rather than being transliterated JEHOVAH; likewise when it was translated into Greek it became the multipurpose *kurios* (sir, master, lord, Lord). But the day is coming when that name, JEHOVAH, a name above every name, will not be used only by a high priest once a year on the Day of Atonement in Jerusalem, but will be confessed by all in heaven and earth, and used of "Jesus".

There is one other possibility concerning this "name" that should be mentioned, and that is, that it is at present *unknown*. In Revelation 3:12 there is a promise given to the overcomers addressed there, that the One who is "coming soon" (v.11) "will write on him the name of my God … will also write on him *my new name*" (v.12). Looking back to 2:17, there the promise is "a new name … *known only to him who receives it*". If the overcomer is to have a secret name, is it possible that Christ has also, to be made known when all in heaven and earth confess Him Lord?

## Christ The Head (Ephesians/Colossians)

The word 'mystery' (*musterion,* secret) occurs six times in Ephesians and four times in Colossians.[35] Earlier in this study, I noted its occurrence in Ephesians 3:4, and have used the phrase, 'the secret of Christ', to suggest that the knowledge of this secret **was** known in other generations, but **not "as it has now been revealed"** (i.e. when Paul wrote Ephesians). As he said:

> My insight into the mystery of Christ, which was not made known to men in other generations as it has now been revealed by the Spirit to God's holy apostles and prophets

In Colossians we have two further references that bear upon this 'secret':

> My purpose is … that they may have the full riches of complete understanding, in order that they may know *the mystery of God, namely Christ*, in whom are hidden all the treasures of wisdom and knowledge. (2:2,3)

> Pray … that God may open a door … so that we may proclaim *the mystery of Christ*. (4:2,3)

The secret of God **is** Christ, and the proclamation of the secret of Christ is the proclamation of what has been revealed of Him in the unfolding of the purpose of God up to the present time. And in the unfolding of the knowledge of Him, from that first enigmatic statement overheard by our first parents in the Garden of Eden, 'He is the seed of the woman', to what Paul reveals in the two epistles before us, what has been revealed of Him is always **related to**, and **for** His people. He is never isolated from His creation. What He became and what He did, was for us.

So what, in these two epistles, does Paul **add** to the revelation of the Person of Christ that had not been revealed before? And what relationship does it have to His people? I suggest it is His Headship over the Church which is His Body.[36]

> God placed all things under his feet (this much was already revealed, even in the Old Testament cp. Psalm 110) and appointed him to be **head** over everything for the church, which is his body, the fullness of him who fills everything in every way. (Ephesians 1:22,23)
>
> He is the **head** of the body, the church. (Colossians 1:18)

The secret made known to Paul "by revelation", of which he wrote briefly in the earlier part of the epistle (Ephesians 3:3) and that concerned the position of the Gentiles in this "church", is related to the position that Christ holds as its Head. I cannot go more fully into that relationship here, as that is beyond the remit of this study, which is concerned with *Jesus: God and man*. Here, in what I see as the latest revelation of Christ given so far, He is seen not only as Head over all things, but in that capacity as given particularly to the Church, the Body of Christ. So who is "Jesus"?

> He is the image of the invisible God, the firstborn over all creation. For by him all things were created … He is before

all things, and in him all things hold together. And he is the head of the body, the church; he is the beginning and the firstborn from among the dead, **so that in everything he might have the supremacy. For God was pleased to have all his fullness dwell in him**. (Colossians 1:15-19)

# Part 4:
# Practical
# Considerations

# Part 4: Practical Considerations

I suggested in the preface to this booklet that the *knowledge* of Christ has its counterpart in practical terms in *acknowledgement*. The more we know of Him, the more we will think of Him and (hopefully) the more we will want to be like Him. And whilst this booklet is not intended to deal at any length with the practical Christian life, it would be wrong not to make any reference to it at all. So I return to one of the key passages in this revelation of 'the secret of the Christ' to consider the mind of "Christ Jesus" *as an example*, interpreting it in terms of John's record of just one event in His life on earth. All actions begin with the mind, and just as Philippians 2:5-8 was both introduced and followed with the practical outcome of *thinking* like Him, so His actions in this example from his life demonstrate His "attitude" in practice.

## Christ The Example

The scripture that I believe best illustrates the example of the *mind* of Christ in Philippians 2:5-11, is found in John 13:3-17 (please read); His washing of the disciples' feet. He did this saying, "I have set you *an example* that you should do as I have done for you" (v.15), just as Paul introduces the Philippians' passage with, "Your *attitude should be the same* as that of Christ Jesus". Then we have:

*His consciousness of His own exalted position*

**John 13:** "Jesus knew that the Father had put all things under his power, and that he had come from God and was returning to God". (v.3)

**Philippians 2:** "Being in very nature God, did not consider equality with God something to be grasped". (v.6)

*He became a servant*

**John 13:** "He got up … took off his outer clothing, and wrapped a towel round his waist … poured water into a basin and began to wash his disciples' feet". (vs.4,5)

**Philippians 2:** "made himself nothing, taking the very nature of a servant … humbled himself". (vs.7,8)

*He returned to His original place*

**John 13:** "He put on his clothes and returned to his place". (v.12)
**Philippians 2:** "God exalted him to the highest place". (v.9)

And then in Philippians 2:9-11

*His Recognition as Lord (Kurios)*

**John 13:** "You call me Teacher and Lord (*Kurios*), and rightly so, for that is what I am." (v.13)

**Philippians 2:** "God … gave him the name that is above every name that … every tongue confess that Jesus Christ is Lord (*Kurios*)." (vs.9-11)

In John 13 we have the Son of God demonstrating the meaning of taking the "form" of a servant, and behind this is His attitude, "the *attitude* (mind) of Christ Jesus", further emphasised in the words: "*Did not consider* equality with God *something to be grasped....* humbled himself" (Philippians 2:.6,8). To have such an attitude as Christ Jesus had, is not to become a different being, but to take on a different *role*. As such He is set forth as an example for every believer to follow.

# Appendix 1: Christ's Resurrection Body

# Appendix 1: Christ's Resurrection Body

What do we know of the resurrection body of Christ? The Scriptures reveal the following.

During the 40 days between His resurrection and ascension, He appeared to many, once "to more than 500 of the brothers at the same time" (1 Corinthians 15:6). He invited the disciples to "touch (feel) me and see; a ghost (spirit) does not have *flesh and bones*, as you see I have", and specifically to Thomas He said, "Put your finger here; see my hands. Reach out your hand and put it into my side". He even ate "a piece of broiled fish" with His disciples. He was not a spirit, and He invited them to confirm it (Luke 24:39,42; John 20:27).

But during His post-resurrection appearances He was not always immediately recognised. Mary Magdalene mistook Him for the gardener and on at least one occasion He "appeared in a different form (*morphe*)" (John 20:15; Mark 16:12).

He also seems to have been able to appear and disappear at will (Luke 24:31,36). Prior to His resurrection, in a vision of "the power and coming (*parousia*) of our Lord Jesus Christ", He appeared "transfigured" before Peter, James and John when Moses and Elijah also appeared "in glorious splendour (*doxa*)". The change in His appearance on this occasion is described as "His face shone like the sun, and his clothes became as white as the light". (Matthew 17:1-9; Luke 9:31; 2 Peter 1:16-18).

Paul compared "our lowly bodies" with bodies that will be transformed "so that they will be like **his** body of the glory (*doxa*)" lit, and in another place spoke of the "spiritual body" of resurrection (Philippians 3:21; 1 Corinthians 15:39-49). Contrasting it with the present "natural body" he said that *the difference* was in "splendour" (*doxa*).

We tend to imagine the "spiritual body" to be something rather nebulous, but Paul's illustration in 1 Corinthians of the sun contrasted with the moon, confirms his point that it involves primarily a difference in *degree* of "splendour" (glory).

In this present earthly body we all "fall short of the glory (*doxa*) of God" (Romans 3:23); a failing that has been taken care of by the sacrifice of Christ and a transformed body in resurrection. Remembering that man (male and female) was made "in the likeness of (God's) image" (Genesis 1:26 *The Companion Bible in loco*) and that Christ is "the image of the invisible God"; "the exact representation of his being" (Colossians 1:15; Hebrews 1:3) and that "we shall be like him", or in Paul's words, "so shall we bear the likeness of **the man from heaven**", it seems that even in our heavenly bodies we will maintain our own individuality and that "**the man** Christ Jesus" will be recognised as "this same Jesus".

If His "body (*soma*) of the glory" continues to show the evidence of His crucifixion (as it did after His resurrection John 20:25,27) that will be a continuing reminder of what we owe Him, the cost of our salvation.

If we cannot relate this rather 'earthly' conception of Christ's resurrection body to His ascension and His Deity, remember the scripture that says, "in Christ all the fullness of the Deity (Godhead) *lives* (present tense) *in bodily form (somatikos)*". The wonderful truth about "this same Jesus" is that He is still, at this moment, the one mediator between God and man, "**the man Christ Jesus**".

# Appendix 2: Person and Being

# Appendix 2:
# Person and Being

The word 'person' derives from the Latin *persona*, the basic meaning of which was "a character in a drama, actor, a mask worn by an actor", hence one playing a part (*Chamber's Dictionary of Etymology*). This is still a secondary meaning of the word today, and we can sense this meaning in the cognate word 'im**person**ate'. It is evident in human affairs that the same man (say the actor John Smith) can present himself (e.g) as Hamlet, Othello or in fact any other male character in a Shakespearian play.

I hesitate to compare this directly with the Being and nature of God (any comparison with God is likely to be a poor illustration) but there is nothing wrong with the conception of **one Being and three Persons**, taking the word 'person' in its original sense. The 'one Being' is God, and He may manifest Himself in three 'Persons' (characters, roles or offices) without ceasing to be one God, or becoming three 'Beings', just as John Smith, acting in a play, does not cease to be *one* being, (John Smith) by 'becoming' Hamlet, Othello etc.

The Greek equivalent to the Latin *persona* is *prosopon*, which in classical Greek also meant "an actor's mask" and then "the part played by the actor". Hence it may include not only physical appearance (how the actor is dressed) but extend to the words and actions of the person he is playing. It has been said that a good actor does not so much play a part but **IS** the part (i.e. **IS** the person he is playing). Hence we may see (e.g.) a play billed with the words, "John Smith **IS** Hamlet".

The word is used in Matthew 22:16 when the Pharisees acknowledged Jesus to be a man of integrity who "regarded not the *person* of men" (*KJV*). Whilst they were being hypocritical here, they evidently had in mind more than physical appearance and what they said was true of Him. He was not "swayed by men", for whatever 'person' they may have seen Him to be, He could see beyond the outward to the heart—He knew what was in man. A much better rendering of *prosopon* is "face", translated so in the *KJV* version some 55 times, and "presence" seven times. In the Greek Old Testament (*LXX*) it is used above all for the "face" of the LORD and in the New Testament of the "face" of the Father and of the "face" of God:

> The LORD make his **face** shine upon you, and be gracious to you. (Numbers 6:25)
> How long will you hide your **face** from me? (Psalm 13:1)
> In heaven (these little ones) angels do always behold the **face** of my Father. (Matthew 18:10)
> Christ entered heaven .... to appear in the **presence** of (lit. before the **face** of) God for us. (Hebrews 9:24)

Behind all these references is the root idea of appearance, not just physical, but how an individual is *presented* to us, hence "presence". Coming back to our example, John Smith may *present* himself to us as Mr. Smith, or in the "role" of Hamlet, Othello etc. He may also be presented to us as somebody's son or somebody's father. In this respect, whilst he may be only one "being", he may be (in the primitive sense of the word) more than one "person".

In order to create, God is "The Word" (Genesis 1:3; John 1:1-3, "God *said*; let there be light etc..."); to redeem He becomes flesh in a body prepared for Him (Hebrews 10:5 "Jesus"); to present God to us as Father, He is the Son, the "firstborn of creation". We dare not limit God.

*The Companion Bible* note on Exodus 3:14,15, "I AM THAT I AM", suggests the reading, "I will be what I will be (or become)" and adds "What He will be is left to be filled up according to the needs of those with whom He is in covenant", so "He becomes Saviour, Redeemer, Deliverer, Strengthener, Comforter & etc". It is a humbling thought, but the various ways in which He has manifested Himself to us, are for **our** blessing and benefit; He has **our** needs in view the whole time, and the culmination of what He has become for us is seen in the Person and work of "Jesus: God and man".

# Appendix 3: Key to Numbers in the Body of the Text

# Appendix 3:
# Key to Numbers in the Body of the Text

**1.** Acts 1:10,11; 2:36.

**2.** Acts 7:55,56. To be strictly accurate it is Luke (writer of Acts) who refers to the Lord as 'Jesus'; Stephen referred to Him as "Son of Man".

**3.** Paul's words in 2 Corinthians 5:16 (*KJV*) about not knowing Christ "after the flesh", must not be used to deny Christ's humanity, for Paul has already said, "henceforth know we *no man after the flesh*". The *NIV* gives a better idea of what he means here: "So from now on we regard no-one from a worldly point of view. Though we once regarded Christ in this way, we do so no longer".

**4.** His constancy in prayer is recorded particularly in Luke 3:21; 5:16; 6:12; 9:18,28; 22:32 etc.

**5.** The word "bruise" used twice here is not the same Hebrew word as in Isaiah 53:10 where "It pleased the LORD to *bruise* him" (*KJV*). Paul alluded to Genesis 3:15 when he wrote to the Roman church saying, "The God of peace will soon *crush* (*KJV* "bruise") *Satan under your feet*" (16:20). He wrote it in the light of Christ's expected early return (13:12). But it is the God of peace who does the "bruising".

**6.** Biblical chronology based on names and statements in the Old Testament alone had long been accepted when such became associated with the name of Bishop James Ussher (1581-1656) and his major work *Annals of the Old and New Testament*. For modern systems on the same basis see *The Companion Bible* Appendix 50 and *Biblical Chronology* by Dr. Peter John-Charles (published by OBT).

**7.** A full list may be found in Appendix 1 of the booklet, *Introducing The Books of The Bible* by the author (published by OBT).

**8.** Is it possible that Eve when she brought forth her first child thought he was the Promised One? It would be quite understandable, even though later it became obvious that Cain was not He. *The Companion Bible* draws attention in a note to Genesis 4:1 that Eve, at the birth of Cain, said literally: "I have gotten a man, even Jehovah" (*'ish 'eth Jehovah*) and refers us to Luke 2:11: "Unto you is born this day in the city of David a Saviour, which is Christ the Lord" = Hebrew *Mashiah Jehovah* i.e. Jehovah's Anointed (cp.1 Samuel 24:6).

**9.** The Hebrews' writer is more concerned with the *priesthood* of Melchizedek than with the man himself. It is possible that this priesthood (pre-dating and thus unconnected with the Law of Moses) was that which was instituted from early times, and was exercised by men such as Job (cp. Job 1:4,5).

**10.** The LORD would not allow the combining of kingship and priesthood and when Uzziah (Azariah) king of Judah entered the temple and attempted to perform the priestly function of burning incense, he was struck down with leprosy (2 Chronicles 26:16-21). Melchizedek and Christ stand out as exceptions to this rule.

**11.** Some have considered Melchizedek to have been a Christophany or an Incarnation of the Son of God, but the words, "Without father or mother" are generally taken to mean, 'having no known ancestry': He was a man. No type that shadows forth Christ can in all respects represent His perfection.

**12.** The Old Testament was divided into three parts by the Jews: **the Law**: Genesis to Deuteronomy: **the Prophets** sub-divided into 'the Former Prophets' (Joshua, Judges, Samuel, Kings) and 'the Latter Prophets' (Isaiah, Jeremiah, Ezekiel and the Twelve 'Minor' Prophets) following (but not including) Daniel, and **the Writings** (the rest of the O.T.). 'The Writings' (which included Daniel) was sometimes called by its major work, **the Psalms**.

**13.** Based on the 'Index of Quotations' in *The Greek New Testament* edited by Aland, Black et al.

**14.** In Hebrews, it has been noted that with respect to the "different aspects of the Christ ….The absence of references to Isaiah 53 is remarkable" B.F. Westcott *The Epistle to the Hebrews*.

**15.** For the relevance of the sign to Ahaz and the meaning of 'virgin' in Isaiah 7:14, see *Tyndale Old Testament Commentary on Isaiah* (*in loco*) Alec Motyer; *New Bible Commentary* (*in loco*); *Word Biblical Commentary* (*in loco*) John D. Watts etc.

**16.** Peter quotes here from the Septuagint (*LXX*).

**17.** 'Political correctness' has affected some translations of the Bible concerning the usage of 'man' in Scripture. It is evident that the word is used in English translations sometimes to denote the 'male' and sometimes to include also the 'female'. To substitute 'person' in the latter case not only sounds ridiculous, it shows ignorance of the Scriptures. When "God created *man* in his own image.... He created him *male and female*" (Genesis 1:27).

**18.** Robert L. Reymond in *Jesus Divine Messiah* Christian Focus Publications 2003 lists the following: Matthew 22:44; 26:64; Mark 12:36; 14:62; Luke 20:42,43; 22:69; Acts 2:34,35; 5:31; 7:55,56; Romans 8:34; 1 Corinthians 15:25; Ephesians 1:20; Colossians 3:1; Hebrews 1:3; 5:6,10; 7:17,21; 8:1; 10:12,13; 12:2; 1 Peter 3:22; Revelation 3:21.

**19.** The Hebrew word *Jehovah* is translated by the *KJV*, *NIV* and many English versions of the Bible as 'LORD' (all capitals) and is transliterated in some commentaries as *Yahweh* (YHWH) rather than *Jehovah* (JHVH). I have kept to the latter in this booklet.

**20.** The booklet *The Divine Names and Titles* (1997) is published by The Open Bible Trust and appeared first as a series of articles by Dr. Bullinger in 1896.

**21.** There is no break in the Hebrew text between the words "A Psalm of David" and "An oracle of Jehovah to my Lord". The custom of placing the title above the Psalm rather than as part of verse 1 is a convenience.

**22.** There are many references to Christ's exaltation to the right hand of God in The New Testament, e.g. Matthew 26:64; Acts 5:31; Romans 8:34; Ephesians 1:20; Colossians 3:1; Hebrews 1:3; 1 Peter 3:22.

**23.** The word *kurios* occupies some 38 closely printed pages in Hatch and Redpath's *Concordance To The Septuagint*, where it mostly translates the Hebrew *Jehovah*.

**24.** It is possible that just as the New Testament parables hid 'knowledge' from some and revealed it only to those 'to whom it was given' (Matthew 13:10-17) so men like David saw in some of the statements in the Psalms, things that went beyond what others were able to read into them, things that we only see clearly with the later revelations in the New Testament writings.

**25.** Psalms 2:7; 8:4-6; 45:6,7; 97:7; 104:4; also 1 Chronicles 17:13. Hebrews 1:5-9; 2:6-8; 5:5 etc.

**26.** Commentary on *The Epistle to the Hebrews* note on Hebrews 1:2.

**27.** John 1:32-34,49; Matthew 16:16; 14:33; 8:28,29; Mark 3:11; Luke 22:66-70 .

**28.** I cannot go into the arguments of some critics that deny the vocative force of *Elohim* (God) here, which have led to such translations as "Your divine throne" or "Your throne is like God's throne". I take the Hebrews' Epistle use of this quotation to express the true interpretation.

**29.** *Jesus Divine Messiah* p. 84 by Robert L. Reymond, Christian Focus Publications 2003.

**30.** This title reflects the *KJV* rendering of 1 Timothy 3:16. The pros and cons of this translation as against that of the *NIV* and other modern versions (based on textual variation) **"He (or Who)** appeared in a body" are beyond the remit of this booklet.

**31.** Some modern commentaries that I have found helpful are *Philippians*: *Tyndale New Testament Commentaries* IVP;

*Philippians*: *Word Biblical Commentary* Word Books; *The Prize of the High Calling* C.H. Welch The Berean Publishing Trust.

**32.** The word 'form' in the English language has undergone changes of meaning since the *KJV* used it to translate *morphe*. Today we tend to use it as a synonym for 'shape' and although it may include that (outward) meaning it does not exhaust it. "It can also mean the embodiment of the form…. The outward appearance cannot be detached from the essence of the thing; the essence of the thing is indicated by its outward form" (*NIV Theological Dictionary of New Testament Words*).

**33.** Reymond quotes from Lightfoot's Commentary on Philippians (reprint Zondervan 1953) and goes on to name other more modern commentators who concurred with this definition; B. B. Warfield, John Murray and David Wells. Lightfoot was a 'giant' in this field in the late 19th century.

**34.** *Reformed Theological Writings* p.49 Christian Focus Publications 1996.

**35.** An excellent booklet by Charles Ozanne, *New Testament Mysteries*, that includes the 'mysteries' of Ephesians and Colossians, can be obtained from OBT.

**36.** A distinction must be made between the Body of Christ in Ephesians and Colossians, and "the (lit. **a**) body of Christ" in 1 Corinthians 12:27. In the former, Christ is the Head, but in Corinthians the 'head' is just one of the members of the body in the illustration Paul is using of the human body. "There are many parts, but one body. The eye cannot say to the hand, 'I don't need you!' And **the head cannot say to the feet**, 'I don't need you!' (12:20,21). In 1 Corinthians the thought is of a 'body' of believers ('a unit' v.12), all of whom are necessary, however 'weak', "for the common good" (v.7).

# Bibliography

# Bibliography

Bruce, F.F. *Commentary on The Epistle to the Hebrews* Marshall, Morgan and Scott 1964

Bullinger, E.W. *The Divine Names and Titles* Truth For Today Bible Fellowship (1997)

Chamber's *Dictionary of Etymology*

*Companion Bible*

Finlayson, R.A. *Reformed Theological Writings* Christian Focus Publications 1996

*Greek New Testament* edited by Aland, Black et al

Hatch and Redpath *Concordance To The Septuagint*

Hawthorne Gerald F. *Philippians*: *Word Biblical Commentary* 1983

John-Charles, Peter *Biblical Chronology* Open Bible Trust

*KJV King James Version*

Lane, William L. *Hebrews: Word Biblical Commentary* 1991

Martin, Ralph P. *Philippians*: *Tyndale New Testament Commentaries* IVP

Motyer, Alec *Isaiah*: *Tyndale Old Testament Commentaries* IVP Reprint 2003

Moulton and Milligan *Vocabulary of the Greek New Testament*

*New Bible Commentary* IVP Reprint 1998

*New Bible Dictionary* IVP 3rd Edition 1996

*NIV Study Bible*

*NIV Theological Dictionary of New Testament Words* Zondervan 2000

Ozanne, Charles *New Testament Mysteries* Open Bible Trust

Penny, Michael *The Miracles of the Apostles* Open Bible Trust

Reymond, Robert L. *Jesus Divine Messiah* Christian Focus Publications 2003

*Revised Version*

*Septuagint* (*LXX*) Greek translation of the Old Testament

Sherring, Brian *Introducing the Books of the Bible* Open Bible Trust

Vine, W.E. *Expository Dictionary of New Testament Words* Thomas Nelson 1997

Watts, John D. *Isaiah*: *Word Biblical Commentary* 1985

Welch, C.H. *The Prize of the High Calling* The Berean Publishing Trust

Westcott, B.F. *The Epistle to the Hebrews* Macmillan 1892

# More on the Godhead

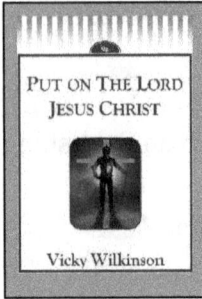

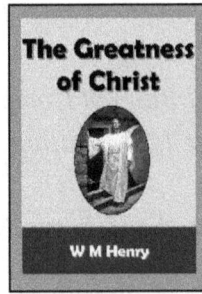

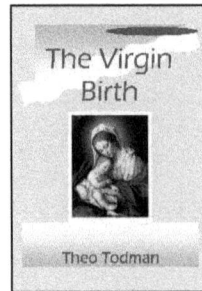

**PUT ON THE LORD JESUS CHRIST**
Vicky Wilkinson

**The Greatness of Christ**
W M Henry

**GOD'S WORK OF SALVATION**
Vicky Wilkinson

**The Divine Names and Titles**
E W Bullinger

**The Knowledge of God**
E W Bullinger

**The Virgin Birth**
Theo Todman

For details of the above please visit

**www.obt.org.uk**

The above can be ordered from that website or from:

The Open Bible Trust,
Fordland Mount, Upper Basildon,
Reading, RG8 8LU, UK.

They are also available as eBooks from Amazon and Apple and
as KDP paperbacks from Amazon.

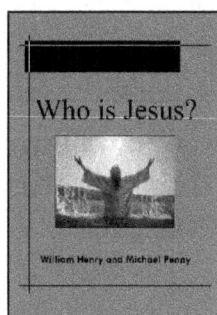

For details of the above please visit

**www.obt.org.uk**

The above can be ordered from that website or from:

The Open Bible Trust,
Fordland Mount, Upper Basildon,
Reading, RG8 8LU, UK.

They are also available as eBooks from Amazon and Apple and as KDP paperbacks from Amazon.

# About the Author

Brian Sherring was born in Isleworth, Middlesex, England in 1932. Following a technical education, he took an engineering apprenticeship and worked for some years as a design draughtsman in agricultural engineering. He was one time Assistant Principal of The Chapel of the Opened Book in London and then spent some 25 years in the food import business and worked with farm animals at weekends as a hobby. He now lives with his wife in retirement in Surrey and writes regular for *Search* magazine.

Some of the other books by Brian Sherring include:

- *Paul's Letter to the Romans: Background & Introduction*
- *The Mystery of Ephesians*
- *The Ten Commandments*
- *The Messiah and His people*
- *Jesus: God and Man*
- *Our Place in the Plan of God*
- *Animals in the Plan of God*
- *Apocalypse: An Introduction to Revelation*
- *The Greatest Love Song*
- *The Song of Songs*

To see a full list of publications by Brian Sherring, and other publications by the Open Bible Trust, please visit

**www.obt.org.uk**

Brian Sherring is also a regular contributor to *Search* magazine;

# Also by Brian Sherring

## Paul's Letter to the Romans
### Background & Introduction
**by Brian Sherring**

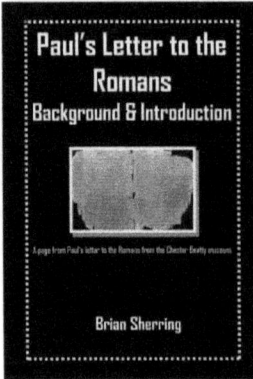

This book sets Paul's letter to the Romans in the context of the New Testament and his other letters. It gives the reader a good basis for a detailed study of the epistle.

Romans was written from Greece some three years before Paul arrived in Rome (Acts 20:2-3). This means that it was written *before* the judgement Paul pronounced upon the Jewish leaders in Rome (Acts 28:25-28). That is *before* Paul wrote Ephesians and Colossians in which new teachings are revealed about a heavenly calling, about Gentile and Jewish equality, and about the abolishment of the Law of Moses.

It is essential when reading Romans, not to read back into it such teaching as these, and the author does an excellent job of explaining Romans in its correct historical context.

For details of the above, and those opposite, please visit

**www.obt.org.uk**

The above can be ordered from that website or from:
The Open Bible Trust,
Fordland Mount, Upper Basildon,
Reading, RG8 8LU, UK.

They are also available as eBooks from Amazon and Apple and as KDP paperbacks from Amazon.

# Also by Brian Sherring

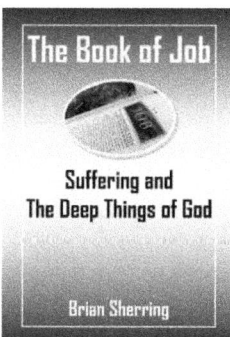

**Salvation**
God's Provision and
Man's Response

Brian Sherring

Introducing The
Books of the
Bible

Brian Sherring

The Mystery
of Ephesians

The Mystery ...
as I have written briefly
(Ephesians 3:3)

Brian Sherring

Our Place
in
The Plan of God

Brian Sherring

**Animals**
in the
**Plan of God**

Brian Sherring

Christians!

Their Message and Their Witness

Brian Sherring

The Book of Job

Suffering and
The Deep Things of God

Brian Sherring

*Music &
Praise*
in the life of the believer

Brian Sherring

Spiritual
Blessings

In heavenly realms

Brian Sherring

www.ingramcontent.com/pod-product-compliance
Lightning Source LLC
Chambersburg PA
CBHW070531030426

42337CB00016B/2180